A

Pony Rider's

D I A R Y

This Diary Belongs To:

_____

19____

A

Pony Rider's

D I A R Y

Nina Duran

Robert Hale □ *London*

To Nona Garson,

my friend and trainer

who understands ponies

better than anyone I know

and to Popcorn . . .

Copyright © 1989 by Nina Duran Suarès

Illustrations copyright © 1989 by Nina Duran Suarès

ISBN 0–7090–3581–0

Robert Hale Limited
Clerkenwell House
Clerkenwell Green
London EC1R OHT

Printed in Japan

Contents

Introduction 7

My Pony's Vital Statistics 12

My Pony's Stable 14

The People Who Look After My Pony 16

My Pony's Feeding Schedule 18

Farrier and Veterinary Care 20

Grooming and Stable Supplies 22

My Pony's Tack and Clothing 24

My Riding Clothes 26

My Riding Friends 28

My Favourite Riders 30

My Favourite Ponies 33

My Favourite Horse Stories, Books, and Films 34

My Local Pony Club 35

My Training Schedule 36

Horse Show Checklist 46

The Gymkhana 49

The Horse Show 73

My Ambitions with Ponies and Horses 93

This Is a Picture of My Favourite Pony 95

Introduction

*W*ithout fail, that first moment—when I'm going to visit my hunter at the farm or I pass a carriage horse in the park and just catch that horsey scent in the air—I'm always brought back to my Popcorn days. Popcorn permitted my first ride on a Saturday morning, with my brother and father watching. He was ancient and, looking back, unbelievably tolerant. Hanging onto his very full mane, I was bounced around the ring a few times, giggling with delight. He very kindly stopped at the gate, waited quietly while I was lifted off by my father, and proceeded to pin his ears flat on his head. He looked fierce, but I understood him perfectly. Out came a piece of sugar from my pocket, and his ears perked up. He got his thank you. From then on I was hooked.

Many of the world's outstanding riders got their start on a pony, taking endless turns around the ring trying to keep the pony from drifting toward the centre (an *invaluable, early lesson in leg aids), learning the art of perseverance on an animal that offers no shortcuts. Watching a seasoned pony carry its young rider, one senses that the pony is doing the teaching. With an uncanny sense of a rider's limitations and often genuine kindness, ponies seem to possess an intelligence you don't always see in horses.*

Ponies also have a superior sense of balance, owing to their lower centre of gravity, and pound for pound seem to be better athletes than horses. It is amazing to see a pony accomplish horse-size feats, and after riding horses for years now, I'm still amazed by how good ponies are.

They seem to come in two varieties. There are the wise, ancient ponies like Popcorn—the sage "belly splinter" ponies that tuck their legs up to their chin when they jump, ears pricked, taking care. They are the ponies that have taught the mothers and now carry the daughters, that keep moving often into their thirties, the only difference being that they are perhaps a bit more set in their ways. But, however stubborn, they remain unflappable, like Lancer, the flea-bitten grey who's taught nearly every-

body at my yard. He's impossible to flex or bend, but he knows the instructor's words by heart and canters on command, giving the rider a thrilling sense of accomplishment that may be false but still builds confidence.

Then there are the imps, the ponies who teach you the art of falling off ("That's yours now," the instructor would say, pointing to the patch of ground I'd landed on.) Pretty Boy was my first fall. And sweet Timmy, a tiny dappled grey, perks up whenever he sees a jump in front of him. He loves to go fast, and the rider who doesn't see his eyes suddenly go bright with anticipation will have a handful in a moment.

But there is a lovely little mare named Rosie at the barn who's the ideal. Neither an ancient nor an imp but a little bit of both, she's a quality pony who's taught her young owner kindness, courage, and a deep sense of responsibility. They adore each other. Rosie always gives her all and never misses in the ring, and her rider concentrates with a child's intensity. It's no wonder they've won so many ribbons. They're a beautiful picture.

— N.D.

My Pony's Vital Statistics

*Registered show name*_____

Stable _____

Breed _____

*Colour/Markings*_____

Height _____

Year of birth 19_____

Date of purchase _____

Sire _____

Dam _____

*Insurance company/Broker*_____

*Policy number*_____

*Type of cover*_____

Insured value:

    Pony _____

    Tack _____

Renewal dates _____

*Freeze mark number*_____

My Pony's Stable

Name_____

Address of stable _____

Telephone number_____

Stable or yard owner_____

Yard manager_____

Instructors_____

_____

_____

_____

Grooms_____

_____

_____

_____

The People Who Look After My Pony

*Groom(s)*_____

   Telephone number(s) _____

*Veterinarian*_____

   *Telephone number*_____

*Farrier*_____

   Telephone number _____

☐ My Pony's Feeding Schedule ☐

Morning:

  Type and quantity of feed _____

  _____

  Hay (quantity) _____

  _____

Afternoon:

  Type and quantity of feed _____

  _____

  Hay (quantity) _____

  _____

Special instructions _____

  _____

  _____

  _____

□ Farrier and Veterinary Care □

*Farrier*_____

Shoeing (Note dates pony is due to be shod):

*January*_____   *July*_____

*February*_____   *August*_____

*March*_____   *September*_____

*April*_____   *October*_____

*May*_____   *November*_____

*June*_____   *December*_____

Special care _____

Veterinary check/Treatment _____

_____

_____

_____

_____

_____

Grooming and Stable Supplies

☐ *Dandy brush*
☐ *Body brush*
☐ *Water brush*
☐ *Curry combs*
☐ *Mane / Tail combs*
☐ *Hoofpick*

☐ *Sweat scraper*
☐ *Sponges*
☐ *Towels*
☐ *Fly spray*
☐ *Hoof oil*

Other items:
☐ *Liniment*
☐ *Wound powder*
☐ *Poultice*
☐ *Water buckets*
☐ *Shampoo*
☐ *Hay net*

My Pony's Tack and Clothing

Saddle _____

   Size _____

Girth size _____

Bit (s) _____

Bridle/Martingale _____

Halter: Stable rug:

   Size _____   Size _____

   Colour _____   Colour _____

Turnout rug: Sweat rug:

   Size _____   Size _____

   Colour _____   Colour _____

My Riding Clothes

Helmet or hat size _____

Shirt:

    Size _____

    Colours _____

Jacket:

    Size _____

    Colours _____

Jodhpurs:

    Size _____

    Colour _____

Boot size _____

Gloves:

    Size _____

    Colour _____

My Riding Friends

Owner/Rider_____

Telephone number_____

Pony's name_____

Owner/Rider_____

Telephone number_____

Pony's name_____

Owner/Rider_____

Telephone number_____

Pony's name_____

▢ My Favourite Riders ▢
(and why I admire them)

*Name*_____

_____

*Name*_____

_____

*Name*_____

_____

My Favourite Ponies
(and why I like them)

*Pony's name*_____

_____

*Pony's name*_____

_____

*Pony's name*_____

_____

My Favourite Horse Stories, Books, and Films

*Title*_____

_____

*Title*_____

_____

*Title*_____

_____

❑ My Local Pony Club ❑

*Name*_____

*District*_____

*Location*_____

Secretary's name _____

*Secretary's telephone number*_____

*Instructor's name*_____

*Instructor's telephone number*_____

My membership number _____

Membership renewal date _____

Annual events _____

_____

_____

_____

_____

☐ My Training Schedule ☐

*Instructor*_____

*Things we worked on*_____

_____

_____

_____

_____

_____

*Things to practise on my own (and to remember)*_____

_____

_____

_____

_____

_____

☐ My Training Schedule ☐

*Instructor*_____

*Things we worked on*_____

_____

_____

_____

_____

_____

*Things to practise on my own (and to remember)*_____

_____

_____

_____

_____

_____

◻ My Training Schedule ◻

*Instructor*_____

*Things we worked on*_____

_____

_____

_____

_____

_____

*Things to practise on my own (and to remember)*_____

_____

_____

_____

_____

_____

My Training Schedule

*Instructor*_____

*Things we worked on*_____

_____

_____

_____

_____

_____

*Things to practise on my own (and to remember)*_____

_____

_____

_____

_____

_____

□ My Training Schedule □

*Instructor*_____

*Things we worked on*_____

_____

_____

_____

_____

_____

*Things to practise on my own (and to remember)*_____

_____

_____

_____

_____

_____

▢ My Training Schedule ▢

*Instructor*_____

*Things we worked on*_____

_____

_____

_____

_____

_____

*Things to practise on my own (and to remember)*_____

_____

_____

_____

_____

_____

☐ My Training Schedule ☐

*Instructor*_____

*Things we worked on*_____

_____

_____

_____

_____

_____

*Things to practise on my own (and to remember)*_____

_____

_____

_____

_____

_____

◻ My Training Schedule ◻

*Instructor*_____

*Things we worked on*_____

_____

_____

_____

_____

_____

*Things to practise on my own (and to remember)*_____

_____

_____

_____

_____

_____

□ My Training Schedule □

*Instructor*_____

*Things we worked on*_____

_____

_____

_____

_____

_____

*Things to practise on my own (and to remember)*_____

_____

_____

_____

_____

_____

□ My Training Schedule □

*Instructor*_____

*Things we worked on*_____

_____

_____

_____

_____

_____

*Things to practise on my own (and to remember)*_____

_____

_____

_____

_____

_____

Horse Show Checklist

Grooming equipment:

☐ *Dandy brush*
☐ *Body brush*
☐ *Water brush*
☐ *Curry combs*
☐ *Hoofpick*
☐ *Sweat scraper*

☐ *Sponges*
☐ *Towels*
☐ *Quarter markers*
☐ *Fly spray*
☐ *Hoof oil*

Plaiting equipment:

☐ *Combs*
☐ *Scissors*
☐ *Rubber bands/Needles and thread/Yarn*
☐ *Step ladder/Stool*

Sundry items:

☐ *Water bucket*
☐ *Hay net*
☐ *Feed*

Horse Show Checklist

My pony's tack and clothing:

☐ *Saddle*   ☐ *Bridle*

☐ *Numnah*   ☐ *Breastplate*

☐ *Martingale*   ☐ *Tail bandage*

☐ *Girth*   ☐ *Crupper*

☐ *Travel bandages*   ☐ *Brush boots*

☐ *Leg bandages*   ☐ *Sweat rug*

☐ *Halter*   ☐ *Exercise blanket*

☐ *Lead rope*   ☐ *Roller*

☐ *Lunge line*

My riding clothes:

☐ *Hat/Helmet*   ☐ *Gloves*

☐ *Shirt (and stock or tie)*   ☐ *Crop*

☐ *Jacket*   ☐ *Spurs*

☐ *Jodphurs*   ☐ *Hairnet*

☐ *Boots*   ☐ *Waterproofs*

The Gymkhana

The Gymkhana

Name of show _____

Date _____

Event name _____

Pony's name _____

Entry number _____

Entry fee _____

Result _____

Prize money _____

The Gymkhana

Name of show _____

Date _____

Event name _____

Pony's name _____

Entry number _____

Entry fee _____

Result _____

Prize money _____

The Gymkhana

Name of show _____

Date _____

Event name _____

Pony's name _____

Entry number _____

Entry fee _____

Result _____

Prize money _____

The Gymkhana

Name of show _____

Date _____

Event name _____

Pony's name _____

Entry number _____

Entry fee _____

Result _____

Prize money _____

The Gymkhana

Name of show _____

Date _____

Event name _____

Pony's name _____

Entry number _____

Entry fee _____

Result _____

Prize money _____

□ The Gymkhana □

Name of show _____

Date _____

Event name _____

Pony's name _____

Entry number _____

Entry fee _____

Result _____

Prize money _____

The Gymkhana

Name of show _____

Date _____

Event name _____

Pony's name _____

Entry number _____

Entry fee _____

Result _____

Prize money _____

□ The Gymkhana □

Name of show _____

Date _____

Event name _____

Pony's name _____

Entry number _____

Entry fee _____

Result _____

Prize money _____

The Gymkhana

Name of show _____

Date _____

Event name _____

Pony's name _____

Entry number _____

Entry fee _____

Result _____

Prize money _____

□ The Gymkhana □

Name of show _____

Date _____

Event name _____

Pony's name _____

Entry number _____

Entry fee _____

Result _____

Prize money _____

The Gymkhana

Name of show _____

Date _____

Event name _____

Pony's name _____

Entry number _____

Entry fee _____

Result _____

Prize money _____

The Gymkhana □

Name of show _____

Date _____

Event name _____

Pony's name _____

Entry number _____

Entry fee _____

Result _____

Prize money _____

The Gymkhana

Name of show _____

Date _____

Event name _____

Pony's name _____

Entry number _____

Entry fee _____

Result _____

Prize money _____

The Gymkhana

Name of show _____

Date _____

Event name _____

Pony's name _____

Entry number _____

Entry fee _____

Result _____

Prize money _____

□ The Gymkhana □

Name of show _____

Date _____

Event name _____

Pony's name _____

Entry number _____

Entry fee _____

Result _____

Prize money _____

□ The Gymkhana □

Name of show _____

Date _____

Event name _____

Pony's name _____

Entry number _____

Entry fee _____

Result _____

Prize money _____

The Gymkhana ☐

Name of show _____

Date _____

Event name _____

Pony's name _____

Entry number _____

Entry fee _____

Result _____

Prize money _____

The Gymkhana

Name of show _____

Date _____

Event name _____

Pony's name _____

Entry number _____

Entry fee _____

Result _____

Prize money _____

The Gymkhana

Name of show _____

Date _____

Event name _____

Pony's name _____

Entry number _____

Entry fee _____

Result _____

Prize money _____

The Gymkhana

Name of show _____

Date _____

Event name _____

Pony's name _____

Entry number _____

Entry fee _____

Result _____

Prize money _____

The Gymkhana

Name of show _____

Date _____

Event name _____

Pony's name _____

Entry number _____

Entry fee _____

Result _____

Prize money _____

The Gymkhana □

Name of show _____

Date _____

Event name _____

Pony's name _____

Entry number _____

Entry fee _____

Result _____

Prize money _____

The Gymkhana □

Name of show _____

Date _____

Event name _____

Pony's name _____

Entry number _____

Entry fee _____

Result _____

Prize money _____

The Horse Show

☐ The Horse Show ☐

Name of show _____

Date _____

Location _____

Indoor/Outdoor _____

Show rating _____

Travelling cost _____

Show requirement _____

Registration number _____

Height measurement number _____

Section _____

Class entered _____

Entry fee _____

Rider's fee _____

Judge _____

Results/Placing _____

Trophy _____

Prize money _____

Comments _____

_____

□ The Horse Show □

Name of show _____

Date _____

Location _____

Indoor/Outdoor _____

Show rating _____

Travelling cost _____

Show requirement _____

Registration number _____

Height measurement number _____

Section _____

Class entered _____

Entry fee _____

Rider's fee _____

Judge _____

Results/Placing _____

Trophy _____

Prize money _____

Comments _____

□ The Horse Show □

*Name of show*_____

*Date*_____

*Location*_____

*Indoor/Outdoor*_____

*Show rating*_____

*Travelling cost*_____

*Show requirement*_____

*Registration number*_____

*Height measurement number*_____

*Section*_____

*Class entered*_____

*Entry fee*_____

*Rider's fee*_____

*Judge*_____

*Results/Placing*_____

*Trophy*_____

*Prize money*_____

*Comments*_____

_____

The Horse Show

*Name of show*_____

*Date*_____

*Location*_____

*Indoor/Outdoor*_____

*Show rating*_____

*Travelling cost*_____

*Show requirement*_____

*Registration number*_____

*Height measurement number*_____

*Section*_____

*Class entered*_____

*Entry fee*_____

*Rider's fee*_____

*Judge*_____

*Results/Placing*_____

*Trophy*_____

*Prize money*_____

*Comments*_____

_____

▢ The Horse Show ▢

Name of show _ _____

Date _____

Location _____

Indoor/Outdoor _____

Show rating _____

Travelling cost _____

Show requirement _____

Registration number _____

Height measurement number _____

Section _____

Class entered _____

Entry fee _____

Rider's fee _____

Judge _____

Results/Placing _____

Trophy _____

Prize money _____

Comments _____

The Horse Show

Name of show

Date

Location

Indoor/Outdoor

Show rating

Travelling cost

Show requirement

Registration number

Height measurement number

Section

Class entered

Entry fee

Rider's fee

Judge

Results/Placing

Trophy

Prize money

Comments

□ The Horse Show □

Name of show _____

Date _____

Location _____

Indoor/Outdoor _____

Show rating _____

Travelling cost _____

Show requirement _____

Registration number _____

Height measurement number _____

Section _____

Class entered _____

Entry fee _____

Rider's fee _____

Judge _____

Results/Placing _____

Trophy _____

Prize money _____

Comments _____

_____

The Horse Show

Name of show _____

Date _____

Location _____

Indoor/Outdoor _____

Show rating _____

Travelling cost _____

Show requirement _____

Registration number _____

Height measurement number _____

Section _____

Class entered _____

Entry fee _____

Rider's fee _____

Judge _____

Results/Placing _____

Trophy _____

Prize money _____

Comments _____

□ The Horse Show □

*Name of show*_____

*Date*_____

*Location*_____

*Indoor/Outdoor*_____

*Show rating*_____

*Travelling cost*_____

*Show requirement*_____

*Registration number*_____

*Height measurement number*_____

*Section*_____

*Class entered*_____

*Entry fee*_____

*Rider's fee*_____

*Judge*_____

*Results/Placing*_____

*Trophy*_____

*Prize money*_____

*Comments*_____

☐ The Horse Show ☐

Name of show _____

Date _____

Location _____

Indoor/Outdoor _____

Show rating _____

Travelling cost _____

Show requirement _____

Registration number _____

Height measurement number _____

Section _____

Class entered _____

Entry fee _____

Rider's fee _____

Judge _____

Results/Placing _____

Trophy _____

Prize money _____

Comments _____

□ The Horse Show □

Name of show ____ _____

Date _____

Location _____

Indoor/Outdoor _____

Show rating _____

Travelling cost _____

Show requirement _____

Registration number _____

Height measurement number _____

Section _____

Class entered _____

Entry fee _____

Rider's fee _____

Judge _____

Results/Placing _____

Trophy _____

Prize money _____

Comments _____

_____

The Horse Show □

*Name of show*_____

*Date*_____

*Location*_____

*Indoor/Outdoor*_____

*Show rating*_____

*Travelling cost*_____

*Show requirement*_____

*Registration number*_____

*Height measurement number*_____

*Section*_____

*Class entered*_____

*Entry fee*_____

*Rider's fee*_____

*Judge*_____

*Results/Placing*_____

*Trophy*_____

*Prize money*_____

*Comments*_____

_____

The Horse Show

Name of show _____

Date _____

Location _____

Indoor/Outdoor _____

Show rating _____

Travelling cost _____

Show requirement _____

Registration number _____

Height measurement number _____

Section _____

Class entered _____

Entry fee _____

Rider's fee _____

Judge _____

Results/Placing _____

Trophy _____

Prize money _____

Comments _____

The Horse Show

Name of show _____

Date _____

Location _____

Indoor/Outdoor _____

Show rating _____

Travelling cost _____

Show requirement _____

Registration number _____

Height measurement number _____

Section _____

Class entered _____

Entry fee _____

Rider's fee _____

Judge _____

Results/Placing _____

Trophy _____

Prize money _____

Comments _____

_____

The Horse Show

Name of show _____

Date _____

Location _____

Indoor/Outdoor _____

Show rating _____

Travelling cost _____

Show requirement _____

Registration number _____

Height measurement number _____

Section _____

Class entered _____

Entry fee _____

Rider's fee _____

Judge _____

Results/Placing _____

Trophy _____

Prize money _____

Comments _____

_____

The Horse Show

Name of show _____

Date _____

Location _____

Indoor/Outdoor _____

Show rating _____

Travelling cost _____

Show requirement _____

Registration number _____

Height measurement number _____

Section _____

Class entered _____

Entry fee _____

Rider's fee _____

Judge _____

Results/Placing _____

Trophy _____

Prize money _____

Comments _____

_____

The Horse Show

Name of show _____

Date _____

Location _____

Indoor/Outdoor _____

Show rating _____

Travelling cost _____

Show requirement _____

Registration number _____

Height measurement number _____

Section _____

Class entered _____

Entry fee _____

Rider's fee _____

Judge _____

Results/Placing _____

Trophy _____

Prize money _____

Comments _____

_____

The Horse Show

Name of show _____

Date _____

Location _____

Indoor/Outdoor _____

Show rating _____

Travelling cost _____

Show requirement _____

Registration number _____

Height measurement number _____

Section _____

Class entered _____

Entry fee _____

Rider's fee _____

Judge _____

Results/Placing _____

Trophy _____

Prize money _____

Comments _____

My Ambitions with Ponies and Horses

My Ambitions with Ponies and Horses

This Is a Picture of My Favourite Pony

A Pony Rider's Diary

Composed in Caslon 540 Roman and Italic

Designed by Danielle Sacripante